TALES FROM THE PITCH

BUKAYO SAKA

HARRY CONINX

RAVEN

For Jenny. Thank you for the opportunity of a lifetime.

CONTENTS

I
OFF THE MARK

June 2021, Riverside Stadium, Middlesbrough, England
England v Austria

"You nervous, Bukayo?" Jack Grealish's thick Birmingham accent pulled Bukayo out of his trance.

Bukayo had been sitting in the same position in the dressing room for what had seemed like an age. He blinked and looked over at Grealish, who had a large smile on his face.

"A bit," he shrugged. "Wish my dad was here."

Bukayo's dad had been with him on every step of his journey to become a professional footballer, and his presence always made Bukayo feel more at ease, more relaxed.

"Don't worry – I'm sure he'll be watching at home," Jack replied, sitting down next to his team-mate.

"I just want to get out there now and show the boss what I can do," Bukayo said.

They both glanced over at the England manager, Gareth Southgate, who was deep in conversation with his coaching staff. Both players had played for England before, and both had had great seasons with their clubs.

But today there was more at stake. Gareth had recently named his England squad for the upcoming European Championships and, although Grealish and Bukayo had both been included in the squad, neither of them were nailed-on starters.

That was why today's match, a warm-up against Austria, was so important.

"Do you really think he'll put us in the team if we play well today?" Bukayo asked, a sceptical look on his face. The England team was full of talent, especially in their positions. Phil Foden, Raheem Sterling, Jadon Sancho, Marcus Rashford … the list went on.

"If we play well enough, he won't have a choice," Grealish chuckled.

"Well, let's help each other, then," Bukayo said. "You find me with the ball – and I'll find you. Get us both in the team."

"Yeah, sure!" Grealish replied, slapping Bukayo on the shoulder. "But if I'm one-on-one, don't expect me to wait around for you to catch up."

"Same with you," Bukayo grinned.

Their conversation was interrupted by the approach of the England captain, Harry Kane. It was still a shock for Bukayo to be sharing a dressing room with Kane. After all, the man was a national hero, even if he was captain of Arsenal's rivals, Tottenham.

"You ready, guys?" Kane asked. "We're going out there."

Bukayo and Jack both nodded and stood up, following their captain out into the tunnel.

For the first time since the coronavirus pandemic, England were playing in front of fans and, even though it was a reduced capacity crowd, the noise was deafening. There was something different about representing your country, compared with playing for your club.

Bukayo looked down at his shorts with pride, seeing the number 7 printed on them. It was the number that legends like David Beckham and Raheem Sterling had worn for England – and now Bukayo was wearing it.

England were missing a number of players from Man City, Man United and Chelsea, who were all involved in European finals, but they still made a good start.

Trent Alexander-Arnold fired over, after bursting into the box. Then Jude Bellingham saw a header comfortably saved by the Austrian keeper, and Bukayo himself had an opportunity.

He lurked at the back post, waiting for an incoming cross. An Austrian defender tried to head the ball away, but it only went as far as Bukayo. He struck the ball on the volley, but mistimed it and sliced the ball into the stands.

"Probably should have squared that one to me!" Grealish shouted, a big smile on his face.

Bukayo and Grealish were linking up well, but the

Austrian defence was well-organised. At half-time, the scores were still level at 0-0.

"I know this is only a friendly, lads," Gareth told them in the dressing room, looking around at each of them. "But we need to show more desire. This is a chance for you all to get yourself a place in the team for the Euros. So let's kick on and get that first goal."

Bukayo exchanged glances with Grealish. Gareth may have been talking to the whole team, but it felt as if he was talking directly to the pair of them. This game was a golden opportunity for both of them that they just had to take.

The moment came 10 minutes into the second half. Grealish fed the ball quickly into Harry Kane, and suddenly England could break. There was space in behind, and Bukayo burst into it.

Kane slipped the ball towards Lingard, whose touch was directed back into Grealish. A couple of defenders slid in, as Grealish and the keeper both made their way towards the ball. Somehow, it squirmed past all of them and found its way to Bukayo, who had continued his run to the back post.

The goal was unguarded and it was straightforward for Bukayo to smash the ball into the net.

He wheeled away in celebration as the Riverside Stadium erupted with huge cheers. Then he slapped the England badge on his chest, not quite sure what else to do.

How do you celebrate your first England goal?

"Cheers for the set-up," Bukayo laughed, grabbing Grealish as they celebrated the goal.

"That wasn't deliberate," Grealish scowled. "I wanted that one!"

"Well, I guess I owe you one," Bukayo chuckled.

The rest of the game was a quiet affair. As with many friendlies, the large number of substitutions killed any momentum, and the game trickled out, finishing with just the one goal.

Bukayo had not only scored the winning goal – it was his first-ever goal for England.

It was something he'd dreamt of as a kid and, in his short career so far, it may have been his favourite moment yet. He couldn't wait to get home and dissect his performance – and the goal – with his dad.

As he was leaving the pitch after the final whistle, he was approached by the England manager.

"You were brilliant, Bukayo," Gareth told him. "It's early days, but if you keep it up, I think there's a real chance you might be in the starting line-up for the Euros. There's no reason why you can't make a real impact."

Bukayo nodded. It was the biggest moment of his career so far, but he wasn't done yet. In fact, he hadn't even started.

The Euros – and the big moments – were still to come.

2

"MOST OF YOU WON'T"

November 2008, Hale End Academy,
North London, England

"We've been stuck here for an hour!" Bukayo moaned, thumping his seat in frustration. "I wanted to practise a few tricks before training started."

"I'm sorry, Bukayo, but there's nothing I can do about the traffic," his dad said, turning to look back at his son. "We'll still make it there on time, anyway. If it matters that much to you, we can always go back to

Greenford and play in the garden." Bukayo's dad raised an eyebrow.

"No way!" Bukayo shouted. "I'm going to be a big star at Arsenal."

"I'm sure you will," his dad laughed. "I'm sure you both will, wherever you play."

It had been a few months since Bukayo had signed for Arsenal's Hale End Academy. He'd been playing for his local club in Ealing, Greenford Celtic, and had been spotted by one of the Arsenal scouts who kept an eye on the players there.

Bukayo was at Arsenal, and his older brother, Yomi, was also making his way in the world of football. He'd been snapped up by Watford, so, as Bukayo and his dad were making the long drive from Ealing to Arsenal's academy, Yomi and his mum were making a similar drive out to Watford.

"I wish we were at the same club," Bukayo sighed.

It was difficult for him at Arsenal. Most of his team-mates were from North London, and those that weren't had come from all over the place to join the famous academy. He'd found it really hard to make friends, especially as everyone seemed to be competing with each other all the time.

The coach's introductory talk, given when they'd first joined, hadn't helped either.

There had been about 30 of them sitting in a room, desperate to get out onto the pitch and play, but instead they'd been forced to listen to the coach explain the academy's rules to them. This was the code of conduct for their future careers.

"I know there's a lot of you in this room who will be looking forward to a long and successful career at Arsenal. I know a lot of you will have dreams of breaking into the first team."

A few of the boys in the room had nodded. They were sure that that was going to be them.

"Well, I say this to all the guys who come through these halls. I just want to be honest with you up-front. I don't want there to be any confusion or any shock."

The coach had paused, looking round at each of the boys in turn.

"Only one or two of you – if that – will make it to the top and become Arsenal players. If you work hard, many of you will still have a career in football, but I cannot promise you that you will make it to the Arsenal team. Most of you won't."

That had been a bit of a wake-up call for Bukayo.

Still only seven years old, he was at the very beginning of his football journey, and here was a coach telling them on Day One that most of them wouldn't make it.

It felt as if he could already see the end of his career looming.

Still sitting in the London traffic, Bukayo's dad caught his son's eye and recognised his familiar look.

"You're still worrying about what the coach said," he said gently, more of a statement than a question.

"I want to be a footballer," Bukayo said simply.

"If you work hard, then you will," his dad said. "You've got the talent. And, you know, if you don't make it at Arsenal, there are plenty of other teams. And if you don't make it as a footballer, there's plenty of other things you can do. Your mum and I will always be behind you, Bukayo, no matter what you do."

Bukayo nodded. He couldn't imagine enjoying any

career other than football. Nothing else made any sense.

"Speaking of other careers," his dad continued, "you'd better start on your homework." He nodded towards Bukayo's school bag, which was lying next to him on the seat. "We've still got an hour 'til we get there, so you've got time to finish off some of that maths."

"Do I have to?" Bukayo moaned.

"Yes," his dad said firmly. "I don't care if you're some big-shot Arsenal superstar – you still need an education. So let's get started. Otherwise, I'll turn the car around."

Reluctantly, Bukayo opened the textbook and began flicking through it. He knew better than to argue with his dad.

A few hours later, Bukayo was back at home, telling his big brother, Yomi, all about his training session at Arsenal.

"You won't believe it, Yomi," he babbled excitedly. "We saw Cesc Fàbregas coming out of the training ground!"

"No way," Yomi scoffed.

"It *was* him, I swear," Bukayo insisted. "Wasn't it, Dad?"

"Well, it did look like him," his dad smiled. "But it *was* dark … "

"Hey, Yomi, let's go outside," Bukayo said. "Just a quick game of one-on-one."

"No way," Yomi replied. "It's pitch-black out there – and you won't let me stop until you're winning."

"Sorry, Bukayo, but not tonight," his mum intervened, standing in front of them and blocking their way to the back door. "You've both got school tomorrow, and it's already late."

Bukayo grumbled, but he knew that his mum was somebody else he shouldn't argue with.

Once again, school was ruining his enjoyment of football.

His mum and his dad were both wrong. When he was a big Arsenal superstar, he wasn't going to bother with education. He was just going to play football.

3
LOSING HURTS

May 2014, Greenford, Ealing, London, England
Borough Cup Final, Greenford Celtic v Chiswick Homefields

"I can't believe you weren't going to try out for this team," Bukayo's friend, Danny, laughed, as they sat at the side of the pitch, putting their shinpads on.

"I didn't think they'd want me," Bukayo replied.

"What? Because you're a big Arsenal guy now?" Danny said. "So you're too good for the school team?"

"No-o," Bukayo protested. "It's just that I don't know

how much longer I'm still going to be at the academy, still part of the team!"

"Really? Surely there's no way they're going to let you go now?"

Bukayo shrugged.

He'd been part of the Arsenal team for almost five years now, and it had become a regular part of his life. Two or three times a week, his dad would drive him out to the Hale End Academy in North London.

He'd get back late in the evening, but before he was allowed to go to bed and get some rest, he would have to stay up and finish any homework that still needed completing.

"You're in secondary school now," his mum kept telling him. "You need to get the grades, so you can't afford to slip behind on any homework."

It had been a tough five years, and there was a part of Bukayo that hadn't wanted to add anything else to his exhausting schedule. So he'd decided not to try out for the school football team, thinking that it was better to divide his precious time between Arsenal and his studies.

But Danny had been insistent, and he'd told the

school football coach, Mr Patel, about how good Bukayo was. It quickly became clear that Bukayo was the best player in the team, but his dad was unsure about the work involved.

"Are you sure you can balance all this, Bukayo? I don't want you to tire yourself out."

"Let's see how it goes," Bukayo said. "I think I can do it."

School football was actually a welcome change from the stress of playing for Arsenal. There wasn't so much riding on each game, so it was more enjoyable, more like football had been when Bukayo was younger.

But today was different. Today was a cup final, with Greenford Celtic taking on another local school. Bukayo was looking forward to getting his hands on his first trophy.

"Alright, guys, gather round," Mr Patel said, beckoning the boys over. "We've done our warm-ups, we've done our prep. We know what we need to do to win today."

Bukayo nodded. The players with him weren't as good as the guys at Arsenal, but he'd formed a close bond with them and he was confident in everyone's skills. He knew they could win today.

"Bukayo, they're going to be terrified of you," Mr Patel continued. "You had their full-backs on strings last time we played them. Keep that up and we'll get goals today."

Bukayo nodded. He'd always been quicker than a lot of the boys at this level, but his time at Arsenal had improved his technical skills – his finishing, his crossing, his dribbling.

All his skills were on display in the first half of the game. Bukayo beat the opposing full-backs every time, but no one could get on the end of his crosses.

"Come on, then!" Bukayo shouted, throwing his arms up in frustration. Until the match was underway, he hadn't realised how desperately he wanted to win the final.

Eventually, Greenford got the goal and, as expected, Bukayo was at the centre of it. At half-time, they were leading 1-0, and Bukayo could almost picture himself holding the trophy aloft, just as Arsenal's captains had done in years before.

The second half got off to the worst possible start, as the opposition fired in a quick equaliser. They followed that up with another goal, then a third, then a fourth. Bukayo felt helpless, watching from his position up front, on the wing.

Greenford got a late consolation, but the result was done. They'd lost the final 4-2.

As they marched off the pitch and were handed their runners-up medals, Bukayo looked over to see the other team celebrating.

Trying to hold back the tears that began to well up in his eyes, he shoved the runners-up medal into his dad's hands and stormed off.

"I'm not playing football again," Bukayo snarled, as Mr Patel approached him.

Bukayo knew that he didn't really mean it. He would play football again.

But he was sure of one thing. Losing like this hurt too much. It was never going to happen again.

4

STEPPING UP

July 2017, Hale End Academy, North London, England

The huge, beaming face of Jack Wilshere stared at Bukayo, as he entered the corridor of Arsenal's Hale End Academy. Bukayo turned to his team-mate, Folarin Balogun, who was walking in next to him.

"It's weird seeing him here," Bukayo said, "you know, hanging out with the younger players."

Bukayo and Folarin had both grown up watching

Wilshere burst into the Arsenal team. They could remember that famous night against Barcelona, when an 18-year-old Wilshere had controlled a Champions League tie against Xavi and Iniesta.

He was an idol for any young player coming through the Arsenal academy – he'd shown that there was a route into the first team, and both Bukayo and Folarin were keen to do the same.

"I can't wait 'til we get to play alongside him," Folarin added. "To train with him, see what he can do."

Since that great night all those years ago, Wilshere's career had been plagued by injuries, and he was currently enjoying a spell with the Arsenal U23s, as he recovered from his latest knock.

That meant that all the youngsters in the Arsenal academy were treated to an up-close and personal view of their hero.

Wilshere proved to be every bit the player they had imagined. Even injured, he showed the little touches and moments of class that had separated him from the pack. Those were little touches that Bukayo was desperate to add to his own game.

For the past year or two, the U15 academy players had been working under the watchful eye of another Arsenal legend, Freddie Ljungberg – a man who'd won the Premier League title without losing a single game.

From the moment that he'd stepped onto the training ground as the new coach of the U15s, Freddie had taken a shine to Bukayo. Hardly a game went by without him hurling some new words of wisdom at Bukayo.

"Bukayo! Cut inside now!"

"Bukayo! Slow it down, play the ball back!"

"Bukayo! No, not there! Cross it!"

Ljungberg was the perfect man for Bukayo at that stage of the youngster's career. Freddie had arrived at Arsenal aged just 20 and had quickly taken the Premier League by storm, playing behind the striker and cutting in from the left-hand side. These were the very same positions that Bukayo was keen to make his own.

On this particular day that he and Folarin were entering Hale End, passing Wilshere as they did so, Bukayo had some specific questions that he wanted to discuss with Ljungberg.

He'd been nervous about approaching the manager,

not wanting to bother him or seem a bit too keen – especially as Ljungberg had a reputation for being a bit spiky. Bukayo had seen some of his team-mates get on the receiving end of Ljungberg's sharper comments, and he was keen to avoid getting the same treatment.

In fact, Bukayo's dad had helped him with the phrasing of his questions, and Bukayo had tapped them into the notes app on his phone.

So, as Folarin turned right to head towards the dressing room, Bukayo paused.

"I'm just going to see the gaffer. See you later, Folarin."

Finding his way to Ljungberg's office, Bukayo hesitated in the corridor for a second, taking a deep breath and composing himself. He had played some big games for the Arsenal youth teams, and when he'd signed his first Arsenal contract he'd even met Arsène Wenger. But, for some reason, this was making him more nervous than ever.

Then he tapped on the door.

"Come in!" Ljungberg's voice sounded relaxed.

Bukayo turned the handle and wandered into the

office, just as Ljungberg looked up and broke into a smile.

"Bukayo, good to see you," he beamed. "What can I help you with?"

Bukayo sighed with relief. Why had he ever been worried? The manager had always had a soft spot for him – there was no way he was ever going to shout at him, as he did with some of the other players.

"I just wanted to see if you could offer some advice." Bukayo began.

"Oh yeah?" Ljungberg said, raising an eyebrow.

"Yeah. I'm just struggling with my finishing a bit, my timing. And I've watched all the clips of you when you were a player – and you seemed to finish so easily."

"Those clips don't show all the ones I missed," Ljungberg grinned. "They only ever show the good ones."

"But you were a good finisher," Bukayo pressed. "I just can't seem to work it out. You've seen me – I can't get any power behind the ball."

"Well, you're never going to be a powerful player Bukayo," Ljungberg chuckled. "*I* wasn't. Not everyone is. I used to place my shots, curl them, aim for the corners."

"Is there any secret to that?" Bukayo frowned. Part of him had been hoping for a quick fix, a simple answer to the problems he had been having.

"Practice," Ljungberg shrugged. "Stay late, come early. Hit the ball at the corners. Or don't worry about it, Bukayo. That's an option too. It will come – focus on what you're good at now, what makes you special. You're one of the best dribblers of the ball I've seen in a long time."

Bukayo nodded and looked away. He didn't really know how to respond to the compliment.

"Are you still at school?" Ljungberg asked suddenly, changing the topic.

"I just did my GCSEs," Bukayo replied. "We get the results next month. My teachers reckon I might get some As – or even A-stars."

"Good for you," Ljungberg nodded. "A lot of kids drop out of school, hanging on to their big dreams of becoming a footballer."

"My mum would never … " Bukayo began.

"Neither would mine," Ljungberg interrupted, laughing. "I even had to go to university for a bit! Can you imagine that? But it was so difficult to do both. You're a smarter lad than me – I'm sure you could do it."

Bukayo laughed. "I think I'll focus on Arsenal," he said. "I'm going to be a footballer."

"Well, I'm glad you said that, Bukayo," Ljungberg nodded. "Because there's some news. They're making me the new manager of the Under-23s."

"Oh, nice. Congratulations," Bukayo said.

"And I want you to come with me," Ljungberg added. "I want you to make the step up."

For the first time since entering the office, Bukayo was speechless. He wasn't even 16 yet, and now the manager wanted him to join the Arsenal U23s.

"If I had my way, you'd be training with the first team," Ljungberg continued. "So go and tell your mum – you probably won't need that education any more. You're going to be a footballer."

5
THE THREE LIONS

May 2018, Proact Stadium, Chesterfield, England
U17 Euros Semi-Finals, England U17 v Netherlands U17

"You've got a couple of options, I think, Bukayo. You could ask to go back down to the Under-18s, and see if you can play a bit more. But you don't want that, do you?" his dad asked, reading his son's expression.

The thought of going back and playing with his friends, the people he'd grown up with, sounded very appealing to Bukayo. But then …

"Well, you're going to have to knuckle down, then," his dad continued. "Try to make yourself versatile, maybe see if you can play in a different position. Otherwise, you're going to end up competing with too many players."

Bukayo's first year playing with the Arsenal U23s had been an eye-opening experience. The pressure was much higher than in the teams below. Players would drop down from the first team, for example, and as they recovered from injuries or tried to play their way back into form, they would bring a new, tougher attitude to the team.

The U23 players were hungrier, more determined and even more ambitious than any Bukayo had met before. They had higher expectations too, and a sloppy pass or a poor shot would be met with glares and strong words.

Even though he was one of Ljungberg's favourites, the new atmosphere brought in by the seasoned pros had changed things in the team. Bukayo found himself playing less and less, and his dad increasingly became the butt of his complaints.

Bukayo had been thinking for a while about playing in a different position on the pitch. He'd already played at left-back a few times, to accommodate some of the more senior players, and it probably made sense for him to try to make that his new position.

The coaches at Arsenal, including Ljungberg, were on board with the idea, and over the next few months he established himself as the U23's first-choice left-back.

The season culminated with him being called up for the U17 Euros, as part of the England team who were hosting the tournament. He was joined by several of his Arsenal team-mates, including Folarin Balogun.

The England U17 team had won the World Cup the previous year and, although the squad had changed since then, there was still a lot of pressure.

They needed to win this.

After easing through the group stage and beating Norway in the quarter-finals, England found themselves in the semis, against The Netherlands.

Bukayo had played every game at left-back and had become an integral part of the side. It may only have been the U17s, but representing his national team was one of his proudest moments. They were so close to a trophy, and Bukayo was desperate to get his hands on one. He could still remember the Borough Cup final when he was a kid. He'd never forgotten that disappointment – he didn't want that to happen again.

The U17 manager, Steve Cooper, was in a defiant mood as he gathered his players before the game.

"The eyes of the world are watching," he told them sternly. "This may 'only' be the Under-17s, but to us, this is a semi-final. This is what we've spent a long time working towards. This isn't the final hurdle, but we are on the home straight. Make sure we get it right."

Bukayo nodded confidently, along with the other players. The Netherlands were a strong side, but he knew that if every player in the England team delivered on the pitch, then they would win.

And that included him, at left-back.

The Dutch team started well, with Daishawn Redan going close on a couple of occasions. Bukayo was finding himself increasingly outnumbered in defence, and he was having to bellow instructions to left-winger Rayhaan Tulloch.

But, gradually, Bukayo started to get involved himself. A vicious shot flew just over the bar, then a driven cross evaded everyone and snuck past the back post. The chances were coming for England, as they peppered the Dutch keeper with shots and began to take control of the game.

But the Dutch keeper was heroic and, try as they might, England couldn't find a way to break down the Dutch defence and open the scoring.

At full-time it was 0-0. Penalties loomed.

"Who's taking one, then?" Steve Cooper asked, looking around. He already had a list, all agreed in advance, but now he was just testing the waters, checking that everyone was still up for it.

Bukayo nodded. "I'm still in."

He was up third, and he stepped up after both teams had scored all their penalties. The Dutch were leading 3-2. A miss now would be devastating.

The walk from the half-way line to the penalty spot was long and excruciating. Bukayo grabbed the ball from the official and placed it on the spot, not daring to look at the keeper – or anywhere else.

He already knew what he was going to do.

He took a few steps back, breathing out slowly. Then he ran forward and struck the ball cleanly, smashing it into the corner.

Now he could look at the keeper. Now he could look around. The ball had found its way into the back of the net. He'd done his bit.

Now all he could do was wait.

Everyone continued to score their penalties, until finally it came to his Arsenal team-mate, Folarin Balogun. His spot kick was poor and was comfortably saved by the Dutch keeper.

England had lost. There would be no cup final, no trophy, for Bukayo this time.

Bukayo immediately went over to Folarin, putting an arm around him, trying to console him.

"Don't worry, mate. Somewhere down the line, you'll get another chance to make it right."

Folarin didn't reply, but Bukayo could see the tears in his eyes.

Bukayo's first trophy would have to wait.

6
NEW BOSS AND A DEBUT

November 2018, Butovsky Vorskla Stadium, Poltava, Ukraine
Vorskla Poltava v Arsenal

"He's been the manager for my entire life," Folarin said to Bukayo.

"So what do we know about the new guy?" Bukayo asked.

"No idea, man," Folarin shrugged. "He's won the Europa League a few times, I think."

"He won it, like, three years in a row with

Sevilla," Emile Smith Rowe added, chiming into their conversation.

"That's good, then," Bukayo replied. Arsenal had found themselves in the Europa League in recent years, after a long period of being regulars in the Champions League. An opportunity to win a trophy and gain qualification back into Europe's top tournament would be a good thing.

"What about young players? Does he use them?" Folarin asked.

Smith Rowe shrugged.

The summer following Bukayo's penalty shootout defeat had brought a lot of change at Arsenal. Legendary manager Arsène Wenger had left the club after 22 years, and had been replaced by new man Unai Emery.

Wenger had acquired a reputation for bringing young players from the Academy through into the first team, and his departure was generating a lot of concern in the Arsenal youth ranks.

It was a couple of weeks later that they got to meet their new manager in the flesh for the first time. He had already introduced himself to the first-team squad, but had now summoned some of the younger players for a meeting. This included Bukayo, as well as Smith Rowe, Joe Willock, Eddie Nketiah and several others.

"Hi, guys," Emery said, looking at each of them. "As you know, with the Europa League and the Carabao Cup, we are going to have a lot of games this season."

The youngsters all nodded.

"This means that we're going to have to rotate the team a lot," he continued. "I've told the other guys this, and now I'm telling you. You guys are my youngsters. You might not play in the Premier League yet, but you will play in the other competitions if you work hard."

Bukayo couldn't hide his smile. He didn't expect to play in the Premier League yet, but first-team opportunities in other competitions was something to get excited about.

"Even though I have a first-team squad that I'm going to use in the league, that doesn't mean there isn't room for the squad to change," Emery added. "I don't believe in picking a team based on name alone. If you play well in the opportunities you're given, there's no reason why you can't get into the Premier League squad."

"Do you believe him?" Joe Willock asked Bukayo, after the meeting. Willock didn't look too excited.

"He seemed legit to me!" Bukayo replied.

"I'm not sure," Smith Rowe added. "He might just be saying it to keep us happy."

For a while, Bukayo had felt that he was ready for top-level professional football, ready to play for the first team.

And now it looked as if the new manager would be giving him the opportunity to prove just that.

His dream was going to become a reality.

Bukayo looked at Smith Rowe. "Time will tell," he grinned.

"Whatever happens, just give a hundred per cent and make sure you really go for it," Bukayo's dad told him on the phone, a few hours before kick-off. "Even if you don't get a single touch of the ball, make sure you're the hardest-working player on the pitch. You can be sure the manager will notice that."

With qualification from the Europa League group

stage already secured, and with a long away trip to Ukraine on the horizon, Emery had chosen to rest a number of Arsenal's first-team players and save them the trip.

Bukayo had been called up and, although he was on the bench for the start, he was optimistic he would get on.

He'd always imagined that, for his first Arsenal game, his family would be in attendance and they'd all be watching closely. But the trip to Ukraine had been too far and they'd been unable to make it.

As Bukayo was sitting on the bench watching the game play out, his dad's words were running through his mind, when he heard Unai Emery's voice.

"Bukayo! Get warmed up – you're coming on."

Arsenal were leading 3-0 and the game was all but won. His team-mates, Smith Rowe and Joe Willock, had both scored, and now it was Bukayo's turn to get on the pitch.

"There's 20 minutes left, Bukayo," Emery told him. "Just get out there and see what you can do. There's no pressure on you – just go for whatever you want."

He was replacing long-term Arsenal midfielder Aaron Ramsey, who leaned in to Bukayo as they high-fived on the touchline.

"Go on, Bukayo," he said. "Go and get a goal. I've got faith."

Bukayo wanted nothing more than to score, but he was coming on at left-back, instead of the attacking role that he was used to.

He didn't really mind. At last, he was on the pitch with the Arsenal first team, feeling a mixture of satisfaction and determination to prove that he belonged at this level.

But the 25 minutes that Bukayo was on the pitch felt far too short. He had a few nice touches on the ball, but not in the attacking positions he wanted to be in.

Arsenal won the game 3-0, to secure top spot in their Europa League group, but the result didn't matter to Bukayo. He was an Arsenal player now. He'd made his debut for the first team.

Now he needed to prove to the manager that he was good enough to play every week.

7
ALL ABOUT PRACTICE

December 2018, Arsenal Training Centre,
North London, England

"Hey, Pierre," Bukayo called over, as the team's star striker did some keepie-uppies.

"Bukayo!" Aubameyang laughed. "What's up?"

Now that Bukayo was training regularly with the first team, he wanted to learn as much as possible from the team's more experienced players. He was particularly interested in learning from Arsenal's record signing,

Pierre-Emerick Aubameyang. To play effectively as a winger, Bukayo knew that he needed to become more prolific in front of goal – and there wasn't a better goalscorer at the club than Aubameyang.

Pierre-Emerick always seemed very cheerful in training, and Bukayo was worried about coming across as too serious.

"I want to score more goals," he said nervously. "Every time I get an opportunity, I seem to scuff it, or hit it wide. But you seem to score with every chance you get."

Aubameyang chuckled, and Bukayo could sense that he was going to say the same thing that Ljungberg told him a couple of years ago. "Practice."

"I know, I know – it's not actually *every* time," Bukayo added quickly. "But definitely more than I do."

"You're left-footed, right?" Aubameyang said, as he stopped his keepie-uppies and started walking towards one of the training ground pitches, all the time dribbling a ball under his feet.

"Yeah."

"Well, I like coming inside from the left wing onto my right foot," Aubameyang said, "opening up the body and curling it into the far corner. It's not the easiest thing to do, but if you can master it, then the keeper will have to stretch to save it.

"What I like to do is have specific shots that I do in specific situations," Aubameyang continued. "For example, if I'm in the box, I usually hit it hard and low."

Bukayo nodded, eager for more.

"In your case … " The Gabonese striker paused. "If you're coming inside from the left wing, try and get it back onto your left foot, then hit it hard and low, if you're inside the box. Try and go across the keeper, towards the far post."

"And if I'm coming in from the right?"

"That might be easier, because you can curl it into the far post. I think the far corner is always best to aim for if you're unsure. Keepers will cover the near post tightly. Because you're left-footed, what you'd do on each wing is the opposite of what I'd do."

Bukayo paused as Aubameyang passed him the ball.

"At the end of the day, it's about practice," Aubameyang said. "That's the only way you're going to get better."

8

THE LEAGUE

January 2019, Emirates Stadium, London, England
Arsenal v Fulham

"If I play in the Prem, it'll make it the perfect season," Bukayo said.

"Are you sure?" his dad asked him. "What if you had to choose? Would you rather have five minutes at the end of a Premier League game, or 90 minutes in the Europa League?"

"Five in the Prem, for sure," Bukayo replied, without

hesitation. "It's the bigger competition, the one everybody is watching."

As it turned out, the Europa League hadn't been Bukayo's springboard into the Arsenal first team. He'd made his full debut in the very next Europa League game, and then he'd played the full 90 minutes in a 1-0 win against Qarabag.

But he was yet to get on the pitch in a Premier League game. He'd been on the bench for games against Burnley and Liverpool, and he was sure he was close to getting onto the pitch.

With the busy Christmas period coming up, Emery would probably need to rotate the team, resting some players and perhaps giving players like Bukayo a chance.

The next game was at home against Fulham, and Bukayo was continuing to train with the first team in the build-up to it.

He started the game on the bench, but with 10 minutes of the match left – and with Arsenal 4-1 up – Emery called him over.

"Bukayo! Come on!"

Bukayo jogged over, taking his substitute's bib off.

"Same as you've done before," Emery told him. "Work hard, keep running – see if you can get a goal. We've won the game, so no pressure."

Replacing another Arsenal youth team graduate, Alex Iwobi, Bukayo spent the next 10 minutes running as hard as he could.

At the final whistle, he came off the pitch without having touched the ball once. Not. Even. Once.

But, even so, he had a big smile on his face. At just 17 years old, he was a Premier League player. Now, at last, he had *really* started his football career.

9
CENTRE-STAGE

September 2019, Deutsche Bank Park, Frankfurt, Germany
Eintracht Frankfurt v Arsenal

"Did you see that stat about you, Bukayo?" Joe Willock teased. "Apparently your shirt number was the highest number in Prem history."

"Whatever, man," Bukayo laughed. "At least I'm already in the history books."

"Maybe one day you'll get the actual number 7 shirt," Smith Rowe added.

"And maybe you'll have the number 10!" Bukayo replied, rolling his eyes.

Bukayo's Premier League debut against Fulham had been his first and last Premier League appearance of the season. Although he was part of the Arsenal squad that made it to the Europa League final, he'd only been able to watch from the sidelines as Arsenal were thumped 4-1 by Chelsea – missing out on the chance of winning their first European trophy.

Heading into the new season, Bukayo's shirt number had changed from 87 to 77. It meant that he was still in Arsenal's plans – or, at least, enough that they had bothered to change his shirt number.

This was confirmed by Unai Emery, not long before the season began.

"I'm not going to look for a loan for you this season, Bukayo," he said, pausing to gauge Bukayo's reaction.

"Thanks, boss," Bukayo answered with a smile. His dad had always told him to be polite and to smile when speaking to managers and coaches.

He'd also told him to be firm in expressing what his wishes were. So Bukayo had come into the meeting prepared to argue his case – that he should remain with the Arsenal squad.

"Do you want to know why we're not loaning you out?" Emery asked him.

Bukayo nodded.

"I think there's a chance you might get into the first team this year, Bukayo," he said. "There's potentially a spot for you – if you can take it. Your opportunity *will* come, Bukayo. Just be ready."

The opportunity came just a month into the new season. Once again, Arsenal found themselves in the Europa League, and the opportunities for rotation were going to come thick and fast.

The first game of their new Europa League season was away against Eintracht Frankfurt – the toughest game of the group stage.

"Bukayo, you'll be lining up in the front three, behind Auba – with Willock and Smith Rowe," Emery told him. "Use your pace, your energy, press them constantly. You'll get chances."

Bukayo started well, driving down the left-hand side and skipping past a couple of defenders, before whipping in a cross that evaded everyone in the box. It found Torreira at the back post, but his shot flew over the bar.

"Keep doing that, Bukayo!" Aubameyang shouted to him. "Brilliant work!"

Bukayo, Willock and Smith Rowe all had chances to score, but the game remained deadlocked at 0-0.

Then, a few minutes before half-time, the moment came. Bukayo flicked the ball into Willock, who sprinted into the box, before cutting inside and looping a shot into the top corner.

GOAL!

"Remember when we were doing that for the Under-23s?" Bukayo laughed. It seemed crazy that the pair of them were now linking up for the Arsenal first team.

At half-time, Arsenal remained just a single goal ahead, although Frankfurt had had a few chances to level the game. The crowd were now getting fully behind the German side and Bukayo could feel their energy spurring the German players on. He knew that the second half was going to be a hard-fought affair.

"You're doing well, Bukayo," Emery told him in the break. "Keep getting at them – don't let the crowd get to you."

"Don't be afraid to shoot, Bukayo," Aubameyang added. "You've got a decent strike on you, and their keeper's not the best."

Bukayo nodded. He was always willing to listen to advice from Aubameyang.

Midway through the second half, Frankfurt were still a goal down and were still pushing for an equaliser, when they were reduced to ten men. This opened up space for Arsenal to attack and play their way through the Frankfurt defence.

With a few minutes left to play, the space opened up for Bukayo on the edge of the box. He flicked the ball onto his left foot and opened his body up. He curled the ball hard with his left foot, directing it towards the far corner of the goal.

It whistled low across the ground, fizzing up on the floor and evading the desperate dive of the keeper, to hit the back of the net.

Bukayo had his first goal for Arsenal – his first goal

for the club he'd been part of since the age of seven.

Arsenal finished the game as 3-0 winners, with Bukayo getting the assist for their final goal.

This was a great victory against their toughest opponents in the group – and Bukayo had been at the heart of it. He'd scored his first goal for the club and had got two assists.

As the players piled back into the dressing room at full time, Bukayo grabbed his phone and Facetimed his dad. The atmosphere in the dressing room was raucous and he could barely hear his dad over the noise of everything going on.

"Bukayo, come with us," the physio shouted. "We need you in the ice bath – you need to recover."

Bukayo couldn't hear what his dad was saying, but he knew he had to go. He raised a thumbs-up to the camera and grinned.

The simple gesture was enough, and they both knew what it meant.

He'd done everything he'd wanted to do.

10
GETTING STARTED

September 2019, Old Trafford, Manchester, England
Manchester United v Arsenal

"It's not as big as I remember it," Bukayo said, looking around at the stadium in awe.

"It's crazy, man," Reiss Nelson said, coming up behind him and slapping a hand on his shoulder.

Bukayo had been to Old Trafford before, with his dad, almost ten years ago. Back then, they'd been in the end with the Newcastle fans – the team his dad supported – and they'd watched Man United run out comfortable winners.

A lot had changed since then. Bukayo wasn't in the stands any more – he was out on the pitch. He wasn't there to support Newcastle either – he was part of a strong Arsenal side. And United weren't the force they'd once been. Bukayo knew that they were beatable.

Despite all this, coming to Old Trafford was still the thrill it had been all those years ago. Bukayo stood in the centre circle by himself for a moment, looking around at the huge stands, which were slowly filling with fans.

He hadn't expected to be here today. Barely 10 days had passed since he'd scored his first Arsenal goal against Eintracht Frankfurt. This was Arsenal's third game in that time, and Bukayo had been involved in the previous two.

He'd made his Premier League debut last week, against Aston Villa, and had only been subbed off after a red card to one of the defenders.

"I owe you a match," Unai Emery had told him, after the game. "You had a great first half and I really didn't want to sub you."

Bukayo remembered smiling and nodding. He hadn't really thought anything of it, assuming it was just one of those things that managers said to keep players happy.

And when he'd played another 45 minutes against Nottingham Forest in the League Cup, he'd assumed that that was the "game" that Emery had said he owed him.

But Emery was true to his word.

"You're starting at United," he'd told him in the week. A few days later, Bukayo discovered that he'd been the first player to be told he was starting against United.

Now there was no doubt – the manager had confidence in him.

And today, he was here, at the stadium, at Old Trafford. The warm-up flashed by in an instant and Bukayo hadn't taken in a single word from the manager in his pre-match talk. He just wanted to get out there, get his first touch of the ball.

Bukayo stood next to Pierre-Emerick Aubameyang in the tunnel, shifting nervously on his feet.

"You're our little pocket rocket," Aubameyang said

with a grin. "Our secret weapon, our little chilli. The boss says you're going to add some spice to our attack."

Bukayo looked embarrassed. "I'll try," he said.

"I've seen you, bro," Auba continued. "You'll be fine. Let me handle the defenders – you do what you do best."

Man Utd v Arsenal was always one of the Premier League's biggest games, and this game didn't disappoint. The start was ferocious, although Bukayo found himself on the fringes for most of the first half.

Then, suddenly, his chance came. Nicolas Pépé was leading a break forward and he slid the ball towards Bukayo. The ball was a little bit behind him and looked as if was going to be intercepted by United's Andreas Pereira, but the midfielder slipped – and suddenly the ball was at Bukayo's feet.

Bukayo paused for a second, almost in shock. There was only one United player between him and the goal – this could be his moment.

The ball was still travelling slowly and he had to dig it out from under his feet. He threw in a couple of stepovers as he moved into the box.

The defender had got in front of him and the angle

was difficult for a shot, but Bukayo dug one out anyway, firing the ball towards goal. It spun along the ground but was palmed away by de Gea. Guendouzi came piling in, but his rebound was blocked by de Gea once more.

Bukayo held up his hands in disbelief. That had been his moment.

"Well played, Bukayo!" Auba shouted, giving him a thumbs-up. "Keep going!"

The game continued at a breakneck pace, end-to-end throughout. Both sides missed chances, until eventually Scott McTominay fired United into a 1-0 lead, just before half-time.

Bukayo couldn't avoid the feeling that he'd been at fault. If he'd converted that chance, maybe Arsenal would have been the team one-up at half-time.

In the second half, Bukayo found himself involved once more. A stray pass from United found its way to his feet and, without hesitation, he slipped it into the path of Aubameyang. The Arsenal striker was typically ruthless, slotting the ball away.

But the joy was shortlived. Bukayo glanced over to his right, spotting the linesman holding his flag up.

Offside.

"No way!" Mattéo Guendouzi was the most vocal, bellowing at the linesman and turning back towards Bukayo and Auba. "That was never offside!" he roared.

"VAR!" Bukayo offered. If Guendouzi was right, then the goal would stand.

After a long pause, with the players standing around watching the ref with his finger in his ear, listening to instructions, the whistle went.

The ref raised his arms in the air, indicating that the goal stood. Arsenal were level!

Not long afterwards, Bukayo got his second big chance. The ball was cut back towards him, coming onto his weaker right foot. He didn't have time to think or change the angle, and he side-footed it, just aiming it towards the goal.

The ball came off his foot and seemed destined for the back of the net, but defender Victor Lindelöf was equal to it. The ball deflected off his leg and over the bar for an Arsenal corner.

Once more, Bukayo looked on in disbelief. That had been the moment, a chance to get a goal.

With ten minutes left to play, Bukayo was subbed off, replaced by the more defensive Joe Willock. Arsenal were settling for a draw.

Bukayo slumped in his seat, expecting a telling-off from Emery. He'd missed two big chances and had cost his team two points.

"You were brilliant, Bukayo," Emery said, sitting down next to him. "You play like that every game and you'll finish the season with 20 goals, trust me. You're only just getting started."

II
BELIEF

January 2020, Stamford Bridge, London, England
Chelsea v Arsenal

"So … do you want to be a left-back?" Mikel Arteta asked him.

Bukayo leaned forward in his chair, thinking about the question.

Unai Emery had departed a month ago, after a series of disappointing results, and he'd been replaced temporarily by Freddie Ljungberg, another ex-Arsenal player and the man who'd been Bukayo's coach during his time in the Arsenal youth team.

Ljungberg's first job had been to address a number of injury concerns in the Arsenal team, especially at the back. Kieran Tierney and Sead Kolašinac were both out, leaving the Gunners with no first-choice left-backs.

For Ljungberg, finding a new left-back had been easy. Bukayo was the only man for the job – the only man the manager trusted enough to fill in for the injured players.

And now, Arsenal had appointed Mikel Arteta as their new manager. He'd been a former Arsenal midfielder himself, and had spent the last couple of years as an assistant to Pep Guardiola at Manchester City.

"I know you've been playing at left-back for the last few games," Arteta continued. "I saw the game against Everton, and I was impressed."

Bukayo smiled, acknowledging the compliment.

"Look, Bukayo," Arteta said, leaning back in his chair. "I'm the new guy here. At the moment, I don't know anyone in this squad. I don't know their personalities, I don't know their strengths, I don't know where they want to play – or where they don't."

He paused and looked across at Bukayo. "So this is your opportunity to tell me now. Help me out. Whatever your answer, I'll probably stick with you at left-back over the next few games, just because of injuries. But what I want to know is, do you see yourself there permanently? Or do you want to go back to being a winger?"

Bukayo paused as the question hung in the air. He knew which position he preferred, but he wanted to be cautious.

His dad had always told him to go along with what the manager wants, to work hard and get yourself in the team, no matter what. Bukayo didn't want to upset Arteta straight away and lose his place in the starting line-up.

But the truth was, Bukayo didn't want to be a left-back – not permanently, not for the rest of his career, anyway.

"There are no wrong answers, Bukayo," Arteta said, and Bukayo realised he'd been quiet for a while.

"Er … "

"You don't want to be a left-back?" Arteta asked, saving Bukayo the embarrassment of finding the words.

Bukayo shook his head. "I want to be a winger."

"Then that's where we will play you," Arteta replied. "I hope you're OK with being a left-back for just a little bit longer, though?"

"Of course," Bukayo replied. "I'll play there as long as you need."

Playing at left-back meant learning a slightly different skillset, and Bukayo's training sessions were different as a result. He was often part of the defensive set-up, alongside David Luiz and Héctor Bellerín.

He would often practise defending one-on-one against his former attacking team-mates, such as Pépé and Aubameyang. Bukayo wasn't a natural defender and, more often than not, the attackers would skip past him.

But he made up for that with hard work. Whenever a player went past him, he would sprint after them and chase them down, until he could win the ball back.

Arteta's tactics weren't too different from those of Emery, but Arteta was developing a more distinctive style of play. There was a better atmosphere around the club too. Whereas sometimes Emery had seemed sullen and disinterested, Arteta was happier and more passionate. He believed in the players, he believed in his own vision, and he believed that he could create success for the club.

His first month had seen mixed results, and going into a January North London derby against Chelsea, Arsenal were firmly lodged mid-table. They were a long way short of the European places, which was where they wanted to be.

"This is an opportunity tonight, lads." Arteta told the players before the game. "We can send a statement that Arsenal are back."

Bukayo was once more playing at left-back, and he felt that he embodied Arteta's new Arsenal spirit. It didn't matter that he didn't want to be a left-back, or that he struggled to defend. Tonight, he was going to work harder than anyone else on the pitch, he was going to keep fighting – for the club.

Arteta's message was tested from almost the first moment. David Luiz was sent off after 26 minutes and, from the resulting penalty, Jorginho put the home side 1-0 up.

The Chelsea fans were in full voice and their team were on the up.

Bukayo was defending hard against Willian and Hudson-Odoi, getting in several blocks and tackles and helping maintain the one-goal difference.

"We can still get something out of this," Arteta insisted at half-time. Bukayo believed him and, as he looked around the dressing room, he could see faces that shared his belief. The younger players in particular – Gabriel Martinelli, Joe Willock, Ainsley Maitland-Niles and Mattéo Guendouzi – were fully behind Arteta.

That belief solidified when Martinelli grabbed an equaliser, after a brilliant solo run. The belief didn't waver when Chelsea took the lead once more.

And then, when Héctor Bellerín struck a brilliant goal from long range to get Arsenal a 2-2 draw and a valuable point, it just felt inevitable.

It wasn't Bukayo's best performance, and it certainly wasn't Arsenal's. But, for some reason, Bukayo felt satisfied coming off the pitch at full time. It felt as if Arsenal were back. It felt as if everyone believed.

Good things were coming.

12
BEST WEEK EVER

July 2020, Molineux Stadium, Wolverhampton, England
Wolverhampton Wanderers v Arsenal

"I'm keeping you in the team, Bukayo," Arteta said.

"Really? Even though the other guys are back?" Bukayo asked.

"You won't be staying as a left-back either. You want to be a winger, an attacker, and I think that's where you're best. You've earned your place, Bukayo, and I'll be moving you back into that role."

Following the Chelsea game, Arsenal had recorded three wins in their next four games, and Bukayo had been involved in all of them, even recording assists in wins against Newcastle and Everton.

He was now top of the Arsenal assist charts, despite the fact he'd been playing at left-back.

But then the season had come crashing down. The coronavirus pandemic had brought the football year to a grinding halt, with all games suspended.

Like everyone else in the country, Bukayo had been confined to his home, forced to resort to training in the garden to try to keep fit.

Eventually, training had resumed and the date of 17th June had been set for a return to Premier League football, with Arsenal away at champions Manchester City.

But this all presented Bukayo with a new worry. He'd come into the team as a left-back, to cover for injuries to Tierney and Kolašinac, but the COVID break had given them time to recover, and they were both fit again. Was Bukayo going to lose his place in the team?

So Bukayo was very pleased to hear today that he

was staying in the team – and moving out to the wing, where he wanted to play. It was a perfect outcome, proving that the manager now had real faith in him.

The restart to the Premier League season didn't go well for Arsenal, and they were battered by Man City, before a damaging 2-1 defeat at Brighton, in which they lost keeper Bernd Leno to injury.

Despite all this, Bukayo kept his place in the side, grabbing an assist against Brighton and playing another 90 minutes in a win against Southampton.

A couple of days after that game, there was even bigger news for Bukayo. He was approached by Mikel Arteta and Arsenal's Technical Director, Edu.

"Bukayo, can we have a word?" Edu said, leading the conversation.

"Sure," Bukayo replied nervously. Could it be bad news of some kind – although he couldn't think what that might be.

"We know your contract is up next year, and obviously there've been some rumours about you possibly leaving."

Bukayo nodded. He'd heard the rumours himself, even though he had no intention of ever leaving the club. But it was good that Arsenal valued him enough to want to start discussions on a new contract so early.

"How does this sound as a new deal?" Edu asked, holding out a couple of sheets of typewritten paper. "I know you'll need to look it over with your agent and discuss it with your family, but I'm hoping it will keep you here as an Arsenal player for a long time."

Bukayo nodded and thanked the pair. He didn't say anything else, not wanting to commit himself, in case the deal wasn't right.

But later that day, his agent and his dad both quickly backed up what he'd initially thought. The deal was a good one – supportive and generous.

A day later, Bukayo put pen to paper.

"I'm glad you made the right decision," Edu said with a smile, as he shook hands and posed with Bukayo for photographs. "The fans will be too!"

Bukayo was going to be part of the Arsenal team for a long time.

The next game was away at Wolves. Arsenal were a few points behind them in the table, and a win would put Arsenal back in the mix for European football.

Even though there would be no fans present, it was a crucial game, and Arteta had already made it clear that Bukayo would be starting.

Arteta had continued integrating a number of the younger players into the line-up, and today Bukayo was starting in the front-three, alongside fellow youth team player Eddie Nketiah.

"We're going with three at the back again today," Arteta said, before the match. "It's the formation that Wolves are using, and we want to match them. Bukayo, they're not the quickest at the back, so you should get some space."

Both teams had chances in the first half, with Martínez saving well from Adama Traoré, and Nketiah hitting the post for Arsenal. But a couple of minutes before half-time, Arsenal got their big chance.

The ball bounced out to Kieran Tierney on the left, and he instantly fired it into the box. It deflected off a Wolves player and looped and bounced towards Bukayo.

Bukayo bent his body and stretched his leg out slightly behind him. The ball was sitting up nicely for the volley, but it was a difficult chance to control. He knew that he simply had to guide the ball, using the momentum that the cross had provided. If he over-hit it, the ball could go anywhere.

His connection was perfect and the ball flew into the top corner of the Wolves goal, out of the reach of keeper Rui Patrício.

"Come on!" Bukayo roared, sprinting towards the stands, before quickly realising there were no fans in the stadium.

Nevertheless, as he stood in the eerie silence of the stadium, he was smothered by his team-mates.

It was his first Premier League goal and, more than that, it was a crucial goal in Arsenal's pursuit of European football.

"Signing a new contract and scoring my first Premier League goal in one week," Bukayo said to Nketiah, after the match. "This has easily been the best week of my career."

"The best week of your career *so far*," the young English striker corrected him, with a smile.

13

SILVERWARE

August 2020, Wembley Stadium, London, England
Community Shield, Arsenal v Liverpool

"I just feel like I should've been involved," Bukayo moaned to Emile Smith Rowe on the phone. "Can you imagine playing at Wembley in a final?"

"At least you were there," Smith Rowe replied. Bukayo had forgotten that Emile had spent the end of last season on loan at Huddersfield.

The season had only got better for Arsenal. Although

they had missed out on European football in the league, they had made it all the way to the FA Cup final at Wembley, and they'd won it, beating Chelsea 2-1.

But Bukayo had been left out of the team that day, so he'd missed playing on Wembley's hallowed turf in a cup final. Because he'd been part of the squad and had scored in some of the earlier rounds, he did get a winner's medal – but, nevertheless, he couldn't help feeling disappointed.

"At least there weren't any fans. If you're going to play at Wembley, you want it to be packed," Smith Rowe added.

Bukayo shrugged. He knew Smith Rowe was right in a way – it wouldn't have been the same to have played in an empty Wembley stadium. But even so, he was gutted.

"A few months ago, you were expecting Arteta to drop you back to the Under-23s!" his dad laughed, when he'd told him. "Now you're furious they wouldn't play you in the Cup final!"

"I'm not furious," Bukayo protested. "I just wanted to play, I wanted to earn my medal."

"You did, son," his dad insisted. "You scored in the fourth round, didn't you? They wouldn't have been in that final if it wasn't for you."

It was the same as with Smith Rowe. Bukayo knew that his dad was right, but he just didn't want to hear it. All he knew was that he was devastated – and that was *with* a medal hanging round his neck. If they'd lost, he couldn't imagine what he'd be like.

But there was still some good news to come out of the summer. Arsenal had obviously decided that Bukayo was going to be part of the first-team squad – and not as a defender. The departure of Henrikh Mkhitaryan had left the number 7 shirt up for grabs, and Mikel Arteta had personally offered the shirt to Bukayo.

It was a winger's shirt, an attacking squad number, and it was a show of faith from Arsenal and Arteta. It told him they weren't planning any big summer signings to displace his role in the first team. He was taking on the number worn by the likes of Robert Pires and Alexis Sánchez, and becoming Arsenal's first-choice winger.

This show of faith continued into the start of the season, for the English football season's annual curtain raiser – the Community Shield. It pitted the winners of the FA Cup against the winners of the Premier League, and once more it gave Bukayo an opportunity to play at Wembley – and this time he was in the starting eleven.

"You got your wish, Bukayo," Smith Rowe chuckled, as they sat next to each other in the dressing room. "You're starting."

Bukayo paused for a moment in the silent dressing room. Normally at this time you could hear the noise of the fans, as they piled into the stadium, but this time there was nothing.

"You were right, though, Emile," he sighed. "It's not the same without the fans."

Arsenal were taking on Liverpool, last season's Premier League winners by some distance. But Arsenal had beaten them towards the end of the year, and Bukayo fancied that they could do it again.

And, this time, there was a trophy on the line.

Liverpool had the early chances in the game but, after just 10 minutes, Bukayo got the ball on the right-hand side and was able to drift in, onto his favoured left foot. He spotted the run of Pierre-Emerick Aubameyang and picked him out with a lofted through-ball. Aubameyang controlled the ball and cut onto his right foot, unleashing a powerful shot into the top corner.

GOAL! Arsenal were 1-0 up already!

Bukayo had finished last season with the most assists in the Arsenal squad, and now he already had his first of the new season.

Despite the fact it was still technically pre-season, the game was played at a frenetic pace, with both Arsenal and Liverpool getting chances. Bukayo found himself exhausted, tracking the runs of Liverpool's flying left-back, Andy Robertson.

Eventually Liverpool found an equaliser and, not long after that, Bukayo was subbed off. He was absolutely shattered.

He watched from the sidelines as the game went through extra time and then to penalties.

It was Liverpool's Rhian Brewster who blinked first and missed his penalty. That meant that if Aubameyang scored, Arsenal would be the winners of the Community Shield – and Bukayo would have the second trophy of his young career.

The Arsenal captain did exactly that, smashing the ball into the top corner.

Bukayo rose from the touchline, grinning from ear to ear and grabbing Smith Rowe.

"Wait until there's a crowd in here!" he laughed. "The noise will be deafening!"

"I think you're loud enough anyway!" Smith Rowe replied, as they ran onto the pitch to celebrate with their team-mates.

Bukayo couldn't stop smiling. He'd secured the number 7 shirt, he'd just won his second major trophy – and Arsenal had just beaten the Premier League champions.

And the season hadn't even started yet.

14
CALLED UP

October 2020, Wembley Stadium, London, England
England v Wales

"So you're a central midfielder now as well?" Smith Rowe asked Bukayo with a grin.

"I guess so. You'll have to give me some tips."

"I would, but you'll probably have a new position by next week!" Emile laughed.

After winning the Community Shield, Arsenal's league season started with a dominant 3-0 win against

Fulham, but injuries over the next couple of weeks and a 3-1 loss against Liverpool forced Arteta to change his team. That included moving Bukayo into central midfield, to play alongside Mohamed Elneny and Dani Ceballos.

"The boss will probably need me as a striker next game," Bukayo joked.

"No chance! Your finishing isn't good enough," Emile replied, but in Bukayo's first game in centre-midfield, against Sheffield United, he managed to score in a narrow 2-1 win. If he kept that up, it was only a matter of time before he ended up playing further forward.

Bukayo hadn't complained when he'd been moved to left-back, and he hadn't complained when Arteta had moved him to centre-midfield either. His dad had always told him to keep his head down, agree with what the manager said, and play in whatever role he was asked.

Bukayo had been a regular for the England youth teams during his time at Arsenal, and at the start of September he'd been called up for the England U21 squad for the first time.

He'd had approaches from the Nigerian national team – his parents had been born in Nigeria, so he could have played for them – but he'd said no.

Bukayo had been born and raised in England, and that was the country he wanted to play for.

"Do you believe the rumours, then?" his brother, Yomi, asked him, during one of the family's get-togethers at home. Yomi hadn't made it as a footballer himself, and was currently enjoying life as a student at Reading University.

"What do you mean?" Bukayo asked. "What rumours?"

"You know … " Yomi insisted. "There's England games coming up, friendlies. Apparently you're going to be part of the squad – you and Ainsley, from Arsenal."

Bukayo had seen those rumours, but he'd totally forgotten about them. He'd been preoccupied with his adjustment to his new midfield role at Arsenal, and he'd actually been looking forward to a break during the international games.

"So, will you play for them?" Yomi asked. "What about Nigeria?"

"Of course I'd play for them," Bukayo said. "If they call me up, I'll definitely go. England – not Nigeria."

"What position, though?" Yomi asked. "You've played so many."

"I'll play wherever they ask me to play. Right-wing, left-back, centre-mid … " Bukayo shrugged.

"It's good to be versatile," Bukayo's dad said, joining in the conversation. "The Euros are next year and they always want a player in the squad who can play multiple positions. That's your way in, Bukayo."

"The Euros?" Bukayo gasped. He hadn't even considered the possibility of going to the Euros. He wasn't even sure if the competition was going to be on. It had already been postponed for a year, and it was still only October. A lot could happen in the next eight months.

"You've got to consider it, Bukayo," his dad insisted. "If you get called up for these friendlies, you're going to be on Gareth's radar. You'll have every chance of making the squad."

Bukayo nodded, not sure he was quite taking it all in. Barely a year ago, he'd been fighting for his place in the

Arsenal squad – and now it seemed as if he might be on the verge of breaking into the England team. And he was still just 19.

He'd been sceptical about his dad's and his brother's opinions. The England games might only be friendlies, but he really didn't expect to be included in the England squad.

But that all changed with one phone call.

"Hello?" Bukayo said, as he answered it.

"Hi, is that Bukayo?"

"Er, yeah."

"This is Gareth Southgate. I've been watching your recent Arsenal performances and you've been great, Bukayo. You're the glue that keeps the whole team working together. I want you to do that for your national team, starting with the upcoming friendlies."

Southgate paused, waiting for a reply. "Bukayo, are you there?"

"Yes, boss. Sorry, I'm just … trying to take it all in."

"No problem," Southgate laughed. "See you at St George's Park for training."

"So what's it like?" Bukayo asked Ainsley Maitland-Niles excitedly, knowing that he'd been included in the England squad for the Nations League games earlier in the year. "What are the guys like? Gareth? Raheem Sterling? Harry Kane?"

"You don't want to be mates with Kane, Bukayo," Maitland-Niles chuckled. "He's Spurs."

Bukayo had watched the 2018 World Cup at home, cheering on the team as they'd reached the semi-final. Now he was going to be with them, he was going to be part of it all.

He didn't really speak to Gareth during his first few training sessions, instead hanging out with Maitland-Niles, the only person he knew in the squad.

But the experienced players like Harry Maguire and Jordan Pickford soon made Bukayo feel at ease, and he was excited to get going for a proper match.

"I want you to start against Wales," Gareth told him.

"What position, boss?" Bukayo asked, getting straight to the question that had been playing on his mind.

"Left wing-back," Gareth replied. "Is that OK?"

"Yeah, that's good. I've played there a decent amount for Arsenal."

"I know," the manager said with a wink.

Bukayo was playing alongside several other players who were being given a rare chance in the England squad, including Jack Grealish, Danny Ings and Dominic Calvert-Lewin.

"I think you all know why you've been selected, boys," Gareth told them. "There's a Euros coming up, and there's places in my squad for everyone here. Impress me tonight and you might be in my team. Good luck."

There weren't any fans at Wembley because of COVID-19, so Bukayo was able to calm his nerves without the eyes of 90,000 people on him.

It may have been a friendly, but it was still England against Wales and, at the beginning, Bukayo was taken aback by the pace of the game.

After playing the last few matches in central midfield for Arsenal, he needed some time to adapt to playing at left wing-back again, but he quickly found his feet.

Then England found the first goal, with Calvert-Lewin heading home.

In the second half, Conor Coady and Danny Ings added goals to make the game secure.

Bukayo himself had a chance to add a fourth, but the ball was palmed away by the Welsh keeper. He was disappointed not to have scored, but he knew he'd had a good game.

He knew there was now a chance – a real one – that he'd be in the squad for the Euros.

And he couldn't wait.

15
WE'RE BACK!

December 2020, Emirates Stadium, London, England
Arsenal v Chelsea

"Here we are then, lads. Seven games without a win. Fifteenth place in the league and well behind the Champions League places," Mikel Arteta said, glancing at the players in the changing room.

Bukayo nodded grimly. He knew as well as anyone the struggles of the Arsenal team. He'd played in all seven games, including the demoralising 3-0 loss at home to Aston Villa, as well as the North London derby defeat to Spurs.

"But even though the results haven't been going our way, we're playing well," Arteta continued. "I know it doesn't always feel like it, but trust me, we *are* playing well. We owe a team a beating."

"He's right, guys," French striker Alexandre Lacazette added. "We have been playing great football – and this is as good an opportunity as any. We get a win today and we can kick on, push up the table."

"We're actually not that far behind everyone," Smith Rowe murmured to Bukayo. "A couple of wins and we could be up in eighth."

In Arteta's attempts to end the winless run, he'd brought Smith Rowe into the starting line-up, and now he and Bukayo were playing alongside each other. Gabriel Martinelli made up the young attacking front-three that played behind the experienced Lacazette.

"Chelsea have fast defenders, Bukayo," Arteta continued, addressing Bukayo directly. "But they're happy to attack – and they will leave space in behind. You have to try to exploit that."

"But be careful," Héctor Bellerín added. He was the right-back, lining up behind Bukayo. "Don't leave me exposed back there."

"You don't need to worry about that with Bukayo," Lacazette interjected. "He works harder than anyone in the team."

Bukayo didn't reply, but instead just smiled. He'd always believed in hard work, and it was good to see that it was being appreciated here, at the highest level.

The Emirates Stadium was still empty because of COVID-19, but Arsenal began the game as if there were 60,000 fans cheering them on.

In the 35th minute, Kieran Tierney faked a cross and cut into the penalty area. He was driving towards the six-yard box when suddenly he fell to the floor, under pressure from Reece James behind him.

"Penalty!" Bukayo roared, raising his arms and turning towards the ref.

The referee's arm went up and then pointed at the penalty spot. He had given it. A short VAR check confirmed the penalty – and there was only one man in the Arsenal team who was going to take it.

Alexandre Lacazette stepped up and calmly sent the the Chelsea keeper, Édouard Mendy, the wrong way.

Arsenal had the lead, but they weren't stopping there. A couple of minutes before half-time, Granit Xhaka curled a sensational free kick into the top corner of the goal, doubling Arsenal's lead.

"The streak ends today, guys!" Xhaka yelled, sprinting towards the corner flag and celebrating the goal with his team-mates, in front of an empty stadium.

Arteta had few words to say at half-time. He simply wanted to encourage his players to keep doing what they were doing.

It only took 10 minutes for Arsenal to grab their third. Smith Rowe slipped the ball into Bukayo, who took a touch and burst into the box. He was a long way from goal and far out on the right-hand side. He took a quick look up, spotting Mendy off his line and Martinelli at the far post.

Bukayo looped the ball into the air, whipping it towards the goal. It flew over the head of Mendy, but didn't make it to Martinelli – instead, it landed in the back of the net.

GOAL!

Bukayo had scored.

In Arsenal's most important game of the season so far, Bukayo had scored a crucial goal.

"There's no way you meant that!" Smith Rowe roared, chasing after Bukayo as he celebrated.

"Definitely deliberate!" Bukayo shouted back with a wide grin.

Arsenal were not just beating Chelsea – they were thrashing them. If they could keep this up, there was no doubt they would turn things around and push up the table.

Bukayo had never lost faith in Arteta, but now he believed more than ever. They were back.

16
EURO SUCCESS

June 2021, Wembley Stadium, London, England

"I really think we can kick on next year," Bukayo told his dad, after the season had finished.

"What are you talking about?" his dad asked. "Title race? Champions League?"

"I think with a couple of transfers … Champions League," Bukayo said.

"Well, you don't need to worry about all that yet," his

dad said. "You've got a rather important tournament to focus on."

His dad was right. Arsenal's season had ended with a good run of form, and Bukayo had been an integral part of the side, as they had raced up the table. It hadn't been enough to lift them into the European places, but it had been enough to get them into eighth.

Bukayo's form for Arsenal had only attracted more and more attention as the season had gone on, and he'd become a regular part of the England squad for their friendlies and qualifiers.

It had almost seemed inevitable that he'd be part of the squad for the Euros, but even so, the call was a shock.

"You might not start every game, Bukayo," Gareth told him. "But you're versatile – you're a big part of my squad. These tournaments use the whole squad because we'll have injuries and suspensions. You *will* play. If you play well, you'll keep your place."

Bukayo wasn't involved in either of England's opening games, a narrow 1-0 win over Croatia and a frustrating 0-0 draw with Scotland.

For the final game of the group stage, England were taking on the Czech Republic. England had already guaranteed their spot in the last 16, but a win here would make sure that they topped the group.

Bukayo was brought in to start the game – as was Jack Grealish.

"Remember the Austria game?" Jack asked Bukayo. "We proved that we belong here. If we can combine like we did then, we'll do what the gaffer wants and get some goals. You with me?"

"Yeah, bro. I've got you," Bukayo replied.

And it was the pair of them who were involved in England's opening goal, with Bukayo driving at the Czech defence, before eventually finding Grealish.

Grealish dinked the ball into the box, where it just looped over Bukayo's head and found Raheem Sterling, who powered a header into the net.

It was the only goal of the game, as England sealed a 1-0 win to secure first place in the group.

But that wasn't the real story of the game. The words on everyone's lips after the game were "Bukayo Saka".

He had stolen the show. Every time he got the ball,

he could hear the England fans in the ground calling his name and cheering him on.

The Czech defence were terrified to go near him. They didn't want to tackle him – they didn't want to close him down.

"Mate, you were electric!" Jack Grealish said, as he hugged Bukayo after the match. "That Man of the Match award is well deserved."

"Bukayo, you were brilliant," his dad told him afterwards. "You were the best player on the pitch. They're talking about you on the BBC, saying you're undroppable."

"I don't know about that," Bukayo replied, a little embarrassed.

"You'll start the next game, I'm sure of it," his dad insisted.

The next game, as it turned out, was the biggest game in England's recent history. It was a last-16 tie against England's great rivals, Germany. A place in the quarter-finals was at stake, and Bukayo knew that the pressure was on Gareth Southgate to get the big decisions right.

"You were amazing in that last game, Bukayo." Gareth told him, a couple of days before the Germany match.

"Thanks, boss," Bukayo replied.

"The game against Germany … " Gareth began, seemingly deep in thought. "We're going to switch to a three at the back – match them up."

Bukayo nodded. Was Gareth going to include him as a wing-back? He'd wanted to stay as a winger, an attacking player.

"You've earned your place in this team," Gareth continued. "I want you as part of the front three – you, Raheem and Harry. Your pace is going to be crucial and I want you tracking back, supporting the defenders as well."

"No problem. Thank you!" Bukayo replied, trying to contain his excitement at playing in the biggest game of his career – and a huge game for England too.

"How are you feeling about it?" his brother asked him that evening. "Everyone's going to be watching. Dad's so excited!"

"I'm OK," Bukayo replied calmly. "I don't think

there's pressure on me – I'm just going to enjoy it, have a good time. We know what we have to do."

The atmosphere inside the stadium was the most intense Bukayo had experienced in his entire career. The England fans outnumbered the Germans by a huge number, and it was only the English that he could hear.

There was a huge cheer from the England fans as Bukayo's name was announced. His dad was right – people had been impressed by his performance against the Czech Republic. He was the new name on the block.

Bukayo was instantly sucked in by the atmosphere, and he was the leading light in England's attack, driving at the German defence.

England had a few chances in the first half, with Sterling seeing an effort blocked and Kane almost able to poke home. But neither side was able to get a goal, and, on the 70th minute mark, Bukayo was subbed off, being replaced by Jack Grealish.

"You played really, really well, Bukayo," Gareth said to him, putting an arm around his shoulder. "I've gone for Jack because he's less defensive than you, even though he's not as hard-working. It's time to push on, make Germany think."

Bukayo was disappointed to be taken off, but he understood Gareth's reasons.

And the decision paid off, when Grealish was involved in both of England's goals, as they recorded a famous 2-0 victory over Germany.

England were into the quarter-finals and, for the first time in the tournament, Bukayo and his team-mates were starting to believe they could win England's first major trophy since 1966.

Bukayo was ready to make history.

17
GUTTED

July 2021, Wembley Stadium, London, England
European Championships Final, Italy v England

"I can't imagine what Wembley's going to be like," Bukayo said to Luke Shaw. "People are going to be going crazy."

"I reckon it'll be the biggest match there's ever been in the stadium. I hope we both start, though. You've had a great tournament," Shaw replied.

"You'll start, at least. No doubt." Shaw was the

team's starting left-back, and he'd been one of the best players at the tournament. "Me? I'm not so sure."

"Mate, you were one of the best players in the semi-final against Denmark," Shaw replied. "It would be mad if the boss didn't start you."

Bukayo laughed. Shaw was just repeating what Bukayo's family and friends had been telling him.

The win against Germany had kick-started an England Euros campaign that had started slowly with the drab group stage games. They had gone to Rome and thrashed Ukraine 4-0, and then they'd beaten Denmark 2-1, in a pulsating semi-final at Wembley.

Bukayo had missed the Ukraine game through injury, but had returned for the Denmark game and had even been involved in setting up the opening goal.

He'd dribbled into the box and played a driven ball across the face of goal towards Sterling, where the Danish captain, Simon Kjær, had tried to intercept the ball, but instead had turned it into his own net.

The big question for Bukayo was, would he start in the final? It was the biggest game in England since the 1966 World Cup final, and an opportunity for the national team to get their hands on their first European Championship trophy – and only their second trophy overall.

Bukayo's family and friends all thought it would be ridiculous if he didn't start, but it wasn't their opinions that mattered. It was only the opinion of Gareth Southgate that was important.

"Bukayo, I wanted to see you," Gareth said, a few days before the final.

Bukayo nodded. He knew what it was about, but he couldn't read the look on Gareth's face. Was it good news or bad news?

"I'm sorry to say this … " Gareth began.

Bukayo didn't need to hear any more. He barely heard Gareth tell him that he wanted to switch back to a 3-4-3, in order to control the game against Italy. He didn't really hear Gareth tell him that Mason Mount and Kieran Trippier were coming in. He didn't hear him insist that Bukayo would definitely feature from the bench.

The only thing he took away from the conversation was the fact that he wouldn't be starting. He'd been playing the best football of his career, but it wasn't enough to get him a place in the starting line-up.

He'd be on the bench for England's biggest game in over fifty years.

The atmosphere in the stadium made the Germany game seem like a quiet Sunday League match. Sweet Caroline was heard from every corner of the ground and the national anthem was belted out at full volume.

And that was just from those in the stadium. Bukayo couldn't even imagine the number of people watching at home in living rooms, and on big screens around the world.

The game started well for England, when Luke Shaw stabbed home after a brilliant counter-attack. England had the lead.

"Come on!" Bukayo roared from the bench.

But the momentum didn't last, and England failed to get a second goal. Italy were much improved in the second half, and Leonardo Bonucci poked the ball home to equalise.

"Bukayo!" Gareth shouted. "You're on!"

Bukayo rose from his seat and, moments later, was

on the pitch, replacing Kieran Trippier to huge applause and massive cheers from the crowd.

It didn't take long for him to get his break, bursting clear down the right-hand side, before he felt a huge tug on the back of his shirt and fell to the ground. He turned to see Giorgio Chiellini standing over him.

Bukayo knew that Chiellini had no intention of winning the ball, but he was only shown a yellow card. It was a savage introduction to the game. Italy were willing to do whatever it took to win the game and to win the trophy.

But England weren't giving it up easily. A few minutes turned into twenty, and then extra time came and went, with no further goals. After 120 minutes, it was still 1-1.

It was now penalties – the cause of so much English heartache and pain over the years.

"Bukayo, I've got you down as the fifth penalty," Gareth said, glancing over his list. "Is that OK? Are you still up for it?"

Bukayo looked down at the floor. The crucial fifth penalty could be the most high-pressure moment in the game. It could be the moment that won or lost the match for England. That pressure would all be on his shoulders.

"I'm up for it," he told Gareth confidently.

He'd taken penalties before – he knew he could do this. He would be the hero.

The penalties started well for England, when Jordan Pickford saved from Andrea Belotti.

But then it turned.

Marcus Rashford hit the post. Jadon Sancho saw Donnarumma save his spot kick and, for a moment, it looked as if Bukayo wouldn't be taking one at all.

But then Pickford saved again from Jorginho.

Now it was all down to Bukayo. If he missed, Italy would win the Euros. If he scored, England would still be in with a chance.

"Go on, Bukayo," Jack Grealish said, putting his hand on his shoulder. "You can do this."

With the eyes of the world on him, Bukayo placed the ball on the penalty spot and focused on his breathing. All 195 centimetres of the Italian keeper, Gianluigi Donnarumma, stood between him and the goal. He looked huge. The whole of Wembley, that had been so loud earlier, was now silent. Every eye in the country was watching him.

Bukayo ran up and struck the ball hard towards his right. Donnarumma flew after the ball and met it with a strong right hand, palming it back out towards Bukayo.

Saved!

Bukayo lifted his shirt over his face.

He didn't know where to look, or where to turn. As if in a dream, he vaguely felt the Italy players flying past him, as they celebrated with their keeper.

Eventually he felt the arms of Kalvin Phillips wrapped around him.

"It's OK, Bukayo," he said. "You did the best you could."

He was soon surrounded by the rest of his team-mates, all telling him it was OK, telling him he was fine, telling him they'd get another chance soon.

But he'd let them down. He'd let his country down.

He could only imagine the abuse that was coming his way on social media. He could only imagine what it was going to be about, how personal it was going to be.

Bukayo couldn't see how he would ever come back from this.

18
POSITIVE MOVES

September 2021, Emirates Stadium, London, England
Arsenal v Tottenham Hotspur

The penalty miss and defeat to Italy had been the lowest point of Bukayo's career. The abuse and the comments that had followed on social media had been even worse. A sad majority of it had referred to Bukayo's skin colour, and the sadder thing for him was that he hadn't been surprised by that – he'd almost expected it.

But he'd had the full support of all his team-mates,

his friends and family, Arsenal fans, and the rest of the footballing world. They'd condemned the abuse and had shown their full support for Bukayo, Marcus Rashford and Jadon Sancho, who'd also received abuse after their penalty misses.

"You can't control what everyone else says about you," Bukayo's mum had told him, a few days after the final. "What *you* think – and how you behave – is way more important than what strangers think. Just keep being yourself, do the right thing, and the people that matter will always love you."

She had helped rekindle the fire in Bukayo to bounce back, but the most inspiring moment happened in a pre-season friendly away against Arsenal's biggest rivals, Tottenham.

It was Bukayo's first football appearance since the Euros final – his first time playing in front of fans, his first chance to see how crowds were going to respond to him.

Bukayo came on as a substitute in the second half, and stood nervously on the touchline as his name was announced over the PA system. He braced himself for the boos.

But, to his shock, there was a large round of applause. The Spurs fans were cheering his name. They were supporting him from every corner of the stadium.

Bukayo felt a wave of emotion go through him, and he couldn't help but clap back. Spurs were Arsenal's biggest rivals, but here they were supporting him, backing him.

His lowest moment had now created one of his most positive experiences. He was going to use this now – he was going to have the best season of his career, get back into the England squad and go to the World Cup next year.

"We need a win today," Emile Smith Rowe said to Bukayo, sitting next to him in the dressing room.

"If we win well today, we go above Spurs," Ben White added, overhearing Smith Rowe's comment.

A month had passed since the pre-season game against Spurs. It had taken Bukayo a while to turn his focus back to club matters, after the hype and intensity of the Euros. Arsenal had made a number of signings over the summer and the intention had been very much to get back into the European places.

But they'd lost their opening three games of the season, without scoring a goal, including a humiliating 5-0 thrashing at Man City.

They'd then bounced back with a couple of narrow wins, but Bukayo was yet to score or get an assist.

He wanted that to change today. He remembered that game against Spurs a month ago, and how the fans had backed him when it had mattered most.

Today, they were taking on Spurs again, this time in the league. It was a Spurs side that had started the season well, but Arsenal were determined to win today, intent on ending Spurs' good run.

"We can definitely win today," Pierre-Emerick Aubameyang said. "They're vulnerable – and we're back in form."

"Quiet, guys! Let's focus now," Arteta announced, silencing any conversations. "We had a poor start this season, but we're coming back now. Let's keep that going today. We win, and win well, and we can march up the league."

"Let's do this, lads!" Kieran Tierney added.

Bukayo remained quiet. He was focused on his own game, determined that today he was going to get his first goal of the season.

After just 12 minutes, Arsenal got their chance. Bukayo took the ball on the right-hand side, standing up at the Spurs left-back, Reguilón, and trying to draw him in.

Eventually, Reguilón lunged forward and Bukayo slipped past him, then spotted the run of Emile Smith Rowe, bursting into the box.

Bukayo's ball was perfect and allowed the onrushing Smith Rowe to bury it into the bottom corner.

GOAL!

Arsenal were one up. The Emirates erupted as Smith Rowe sprinted over to Bukayo.

"Great ball, Bukayo!"

"Now you owe me one!" Bukayo replied.

Fifteen minutes later, a ruthless Arsenal counter-attack ended with Aubameyang sweeping home to double their lead.

Bukayo was determined to get in on the act. Spurs

seemed to be all over the place, and he could sense that there were more goals in the game.

A few minutes later, a classy Smith Rowe pass found Bukayo's feet, just inside the Spurs half. He had acres of space in front of him and he ran into it, driving at the Spurs defence, remembering the form he'd found at the Euros.

Bukayo skipped into the box, where he tried a left-footed shot that was blocked by a diving defender. But the ball rebounded straight to Bukayo's feet. He didn't need a second invitation to smash it into the far corner with his right foot.

Arsenal were 3-0 up! They weren't just beating Spurs – they were thrashing them. And Bukayo had a goal and an assist!

Spurs pulled a goal back before the end, but it wasn't enough to prevent Arsenal from getting the win and leapfrogging them in the league table.

The season might have started poorly for Arsenal, but their young guns were starting to show the potential they had promised.

Barely three years ago, Bukayo hadn't even been in

the U23 squad. Now he was a regular for Arsenal and England.

And also, with hindsight, he could even see how that terrible penalty miss against Italy had made him a better player, a stronger person.

He couldn't wait to see where this season was going to take him.

19

REACHING FOR THE STARS

December 2021, Carrow Road, Norwich, England
Norwich City v Arsenal

"We can extend our winning streak to four today, lads! If we want to finish in the top four, then these are the kinds of runs we need to put together!" Granit Xhaka shouted in the dressing room.

After a 5-1 win in the League Cup quarter-finals against Sunderland, spirits were high in North London. Bukayo was confident that the team were heading in the right direction and, now that they were within touching distance of the top four, he was dreaming of Champions League football next season.

"These are the kind of matches we have to be winning," Emile Smith Rowe said to Bukayo, referring to Norwich's lowly position in the table.

"I know. It's a good thing I can feel goals coming today."

In addition to four assists and the goal Bukayo had scored against Spurs, he'd only scored one other Premier League goal all season – but it had come in Arsenal's last league match against Leeds, and Bukayo was keen to score in consecutive games.

Norwich were fighting to avoid relegation, so the crowd under the lights at Carrow Road was energetic.

After only six minutes, Arsenal got off to the perfect start.

On the counter-attack, Martin Ødegaard laid the ball off to Bukayo on the right-hand side of the box.

He took two quick touches, before flicking the ball onto his left foot and curling it towards the far corner.

GOAL!

Bukayo jogged away, before knee-sliding and turning to the Arsenal fans in the crowd.

"I guess your feeling was right!" Smith Rowe said, hugging Bukayo.

"I'm not stopping there, though," Bukayo replied. He'd never been hungrier to score goals.

Then Kieran Tierney scored a second for Arsenal, giving them a comfortable margin.

On the hour mark, Bukayo received the ball from Lacazette on the right-hand edge of the box. He beat his defender, dribbling past him into the middle of the pitch, and then unleashed a shot towards the bottom-left corner.

It fizzed and bounced past the keeper, who had no chance.

GOAL!

"That has to be one of the best goals of your career!" Lacazette said to Bukayo as they celebrated.

Not only had Bukayo scored in consecutive Premier League games – he'd also scored the first brace of his career.

Late in the game, Lacazette and Smith Rowe added

two more goals to secure an emphatic 5-0 win for Arsenal. They were streaking towards the top four, right where Bukayo knew they belonged.

As he walked off the pitch to applause from the away end, Bukayo couldn't help but think about how far he'd come.

He could see the World Cup coming up in 2022 and he was determined to keep his place in the England starting line-up.

He was going to make amends for the Euros, and he was going to repay the faith the footballing world had shown in him.

And he was still only 20. He'd done so much in his career already, yet he knew he was still going to do so much more.

HOW MANY
HAVE YOU READ?